The Speech
A Guide to Effective Speaking

By the Faculty in Effective Speaking at
Cazenovia College

Kathryn Barbour, Ph.D.
Maryrose Eannace
Tim Emerson
John Robert Greene, Ph.D.
Paul MacArthur
Margot Papworth
Carol Radin
John Suarez

KENDALL/HUNT PUBLISHING COMPANY
2460 Kerper Boulevard   P.O. Box 539   Dubuque, Iowa 52004-0539

Dedicated to our Students

CONTENTS

Acknowledgements

No book is written in a vacuum. People helped us finish this work, and we would be remiss if we did not thank them.

First we would like to thank each other. As was our previous book, *The Quest: A Guide to the Job Interview*, this was a collaborative effort, and we spent the better part of a year reading each others work, analyzing it, testing it in our classes, and offering each other our criticism. We weren't always kind to each other's ideas, but our comments to each other made for a better book. We made a pretty good team.

Our spouses, significant others, children, and other members of our families gave us the time to work, and the distance to work *right*.

The faculty and administration of Cazenovia College supported our efforts at every turn. Let us acknowledge the special contributions to this volume of college President Steven Schneeweiss, Vice President Carolyn B. Ware, Vice President Adelaide Van Titus, Faith Dickenson, and Virginia Solomon.

The burden of preparing the manuscript was shared by Sarah Vander Voort and Linda Eno. The figures in Chapter Four were prepared by Amy Wagner. Photo Credits are with Sheila Krux Photography, Fayetteville, New York.

Finally, to our students—those who we have taught, and those who will learn something from this book. It is to you that our work is once again dedicated, as it should be. We wrote this for you, and few things have given us more pleasure as professors. Find your measure of success, earn it, and we will have succeeded as teachers.

Cazenovia College
Cazenovia, NY
July, 1993

"I Already Know it's Good for Me, But Why Are You Making Me Take This Course?"

More and more, those of you who are reading this book as a text in your Public Speaking course are in that class because high schools, colleges and universities are *requiring* you to do so. You probably know that this is in direct response to the demand of business and industry—they have said clearly over the past decade that effective speaking is the ability that their new employees most clearly *lack*. Even if it isn't a rock-solid requirement, you have probably faced a parent or an academic advisor who made it sound like you would be foolish if you passed up the opportunity to improve your speaking abilities.

We may as well get this out of the way from the start. We *know* that you're nervous about doing this. But the authors of this text believe that public speaking *should* be required of all college level students, and we firmly believe that even if it isn't, you *would* be foolish if you passed up the opportunity to improve your speaking abilities.

But enough of such harsh talk. You will see in the next chapter that the above two paragraphs have used the technique of **stimulation**—telling you that you *should* do something. How can we **motivate** you to improve your ability to orally communicate—what reasons can we give you to *want* to take a basic speech course?

- **It will improve your speaking ability.** Alright, so that's the obvious one. However, it is the *one skill that the overwhelming majority of employers surveyed say that*

1

*college students **do not have** upon graduation.* Therefore . . .

- **It will help you get and keep a job.**
- **It will also improve your self esteem.** You *can* speak in
public, no matter how nervous you are. However, the more
often you speak, the better that you will feel about yourself
as a person—and *that's* something worth having.

But perhaps most important, this course will . . .

- **Make you more aware of the people around you.** We will
define it in our first chapter as *empathy*—a commodity
which is often in small supply among college students.
When you have it, you are truly something special—someone who people will *want* to work with and be with.

With your minimal effort and cooperation, these are *promises* that
we can make to you. After all, this is not nuclear science we're
teaching. You've spoken to other people all your lives. Now, however, you have the opportunity to learn to do it *better*.

CHAPTER 2

Who Are You?

Speaker Credibility

Most everybody reading this text has spent a great deal of time on the receiving end of a classroom situation. Stop to think for just a moment—when was the last time that you sat in a lecture, and *knew that the teacher either didn't care, or really didn't know what they were talking about?* Lets face it—it's an imperfect world, so it happens.

If you can see it in a teacher, your audience can see it in *you*, when *you* speak.

Sincerity

The entirety of the speaking situation is up to the speaker. As you will see in Chapter Four, when the process of communications is working right, the person(s) who is (are) "speaking" changes in the blink of an eye. Nevertheless, *the speaker is always in control.* You, as that speaker, *must care about your topic, and know what you're talking about.*

This is not an overly complicated concept, although speaking professionals have assigned it the label of *speaker credibility*. It is that intangible feeling that an audience gets when they *know* the speaker to be believable. This only happens if the speaker cares about their subject, and is as close to an expert on the subject as anyone else in the room.

In short, the entirety of the speaking situation is ultimately governed by the speaker's *sincerity*. You *must be believed, and must be believable, if you are going to communicate with any size audience*. Someone who tries to talk about something that they are either not interested in, or not well-versed in will only bore the audience.

They will forgive a glitch in delivery, a slip of eye contact, or a mispronounced word.

They will never forgive having to listen to a phony.

Hints to Remember

- If *you* don't care, why should your audience?
- If *you* don't know your topic, how do you *ever* expect your audience to understand it?

CHAPTER 3

Who are They?

Audience Analysis

Imagine that you're going to deliver a speech about solar energy. Does it make any difference whether you're speaking to an environmental club or a business organization? You *bet* it does! Environmentalists probably know quite a bit about solar energy already, and they certainly don't need to be sold on its virtues. Your speech to them could center on do-it-yourself home installation of solar panels. Business people, however, may not be familiar with solar energy as a practical solution, and will want to see such things as cost and efficiency comparisons with other fuels, relative tax benefits, savings over time next to installation prices, and back up plans for cloudy days. Clearly, your speech to the business people needs to be an *entirely different speech*.

An examination of your audience will determine the way your speech develops. How much material will you need? You don't want to burden listeners with more information than they can absorb, but you don't want to insult their intelligence, either. What type of material should you prepare? As in the solar energy example above, *a different audience may need to have completely different material on the same topic.*

Researching Your Audience

If you are speaking at a meeting of a particular organization, you can research the organization in your local library. Is it a national organization? What are the goals and purpose of this group? Check local newspapers to see what this group has been doing recently. Are there common criteria that define these listeners? Will the audience be voluntary or captive?

You could also research an audience directly. Survey its members. Distribute a questionnaire at a meeting prior to your speaking engagement. This will enable you to discover exactly what may be important information for you in preparing a specific topic for this group.

There may be times when prior audience research is difficult or even impossible. *Why not make audience analysis part of your presentation?* Plan audience participation that will enable you to discover the basic facts you will need to effectively address this group. If it's a small group, perhaps you could ask them to introduce themselves and tell something about themselves. If you do ask questions and invite participation, be sure to listen to what these people say, and then adapt! Don't invite them to share and then ignore their input. Not only is that ineffective, it's rude!

Watch your listeners during your speech—you can practice audience analysis while you are talking! Are they looking at you? Do they make and maintain eye contact? Do their faces show interest? Are they responsive? Restless? Asking questions? Gather their feedback and respond to it, and you will find yourself communicating rather that lecturing (for further thoughts on Eye Contact, see Chapter Thirteen).

Personalize Your Information

Audience analysis is useless until you put it to work. *Customize your presentation in order to relate it to your particular listeners*. If you do this properly, you may find that topics you originally thought were impossible for a certain audience become strong crowd pleasers! Imagine that you are an expert in microbiology, and that it's your passion to speak about this topic. However, you are asked to speak to a gathering of Mid-Western corn farmers. Will they be willing to listen to you discuss microbiology, whether or not you are an expert? They will if you discuss an aspect of microbiology *relevant to their lives and interests*. For example, suppose there's a newly discovered microbe which, introduced to the soil, enhances the fertilization process and has resulted in substantially greater crop yields in controlled studies. Will they listen? Speak their language, and you'll certainly have their attention!

Show Common Ground

How do you add apples and oranges? Any young mathematics student can tell you that you can't, at least until you find a common denominator—fruit, for example. The same thing is true of speaking. You must show the audience either that you are one of them, or at least that you understand their situation and concerns. *Always speak to people, never at them.* Know your audience and speak their language. Adapt your ideas and presentation to reflect those listeners. Speaking extemporaneously (without reading word-for-word from a script, as discussed in Chapter Eleven) is by far the best way to accomplish this, since the speaker can adjust moment to moment to the audience's feedback.

Hints to Remember

- Know your audience.
- Speak to them in their own language.
- Find and demonstrate common ground.

CHAPTER 4

Communications as Sharing

The Speech Communication Process

There are two ways of looking at the act of communicating. The oldest way—and the least useful—is to think of it as one person (Chapter Two's speaker) speaking to another, passive person (the audience from Chapter Three), who may or may not be listening. When the second person is done listening, they may or may not respond to what the other person has tried to convey. If they do, then the other person may or may not listen to the message. This creates in the mind of the student what we would like to call the **ping-pong** approach to communications (see Figure 4.1).

The problem with this approach is something that can be gleaned from common sense. It is relatively easy to sense that when you listen to someone, you are constantly giving them hints as to how

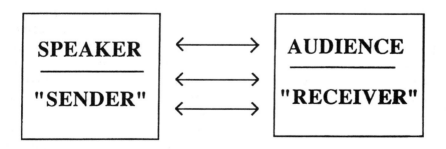

Figure 4.1

you feel about what they are saying—a raised eyebrow, a smile, a word of response—all of which are forms of feedback to the speaker. This goes on *while the speaker continues to talk.* There is no stopping and starting; there is never any magic moment when you stop being the receiver ("audience") and suddenly turn into the sender ("speaker"). *In the act of communications, you perform the roles of both sender and receiver at the same time.* This act of *sharing a message* is how true communications really happens. This can be seen in Figure 4.2, a first step toward visualizing the speech communications process. Note that unlike the ping-pong approach, this one is in the shape of a **circle**. This is to reinforce the fact that theoretically, true communications doesn't stop—**it is a continuous process which occurs between sender and receiver.** Whenever two people are trying to share an idea (or message) with each other, they move back and forth between being the sender and the receiver with the speed of a nerve synapse.

Factors Which Slow Down the Sharing Process

We all know, however, that not everybody "communicates" when they talk to each other. For any number of reasons, a receiver may not understand the sender's idea, or message. A few of these reasons are listed below, and then we will add them to our diagram. First, and foremost, the receiver might not be listening to the message. We'll save a more formal definition of this point until later, but for now, let's just say that it is *theoretically impossible to truly listen to someone unless you're looking at them.* That's because the sender actually sends two messages. The first, the **intended message**, is made up of the words that the sender wants to say—what is in their notes, or what they have memorized. Those words are easy to *hear*—all you have to do is understand English, and not have a hearing problem. However, when the sender speaks those words, they "color" them with gestures, facial expressions, tone of voice, body movements, visual aids, and the like—all of which give us more insight into what the sender *really* means. When you *look* at a speaker, then, you are receiving not only their intended message, but their actual message—the words that they are sending, accompanied by their nonverbal indicators. Once you find yourself looking beyond the mere words, and for the **actual message**, then and *only* then are you actually listening. If you only hear the words, then the communications circle can't be complete.

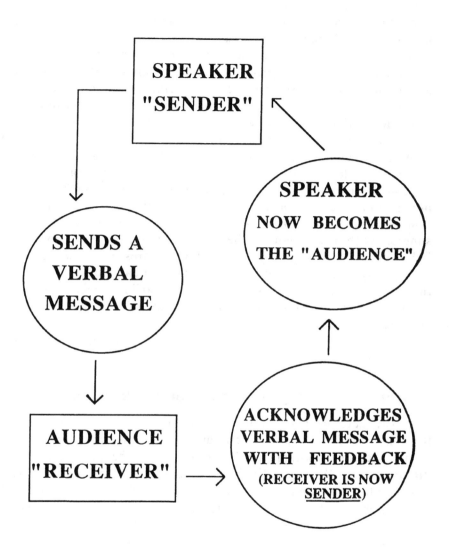

Figure 4.2

One way to improve your ability to listen for the actual message is to think in terms of a commodity which is in short supply, both in communications and in life itself—**empathy**, the capability to feel another person's feelings or ideas. Said another way, empathy is the ability to "walk a mile in the other person's shoes." If you don't stop to think about *who that speaker really is*—their sex, their race, their age, their hometown, their educational training, their complete point of view, or frame of reference—you can't understand the subtleties of the nonverbal indicators which comprise their actual message.

Listening and empathy are both factors which the sender and receiver can control. There are, however, other factors more difficult to control. These are loosely defined as **environmental interference**—factors which *act upon* the communications situation, but are not inherently a *part of it* (some texts call these irritants "noise"). Some examples: looking into the eyes of someone wearing mirrored sunglasses (how can you get the actual message from someone who is hiding their eyes from you?); a sloppily dressed sender; a room with gaudy wallpaper that is *so* bad that you can't pay attention to the sender; or the ever popular sounds of traffic screeching outside an open window. All these and more can stop us from listening—they also can break the circle.

We can now take a look at our improved diagram, which includes these negative factors (see Figure 4.3).

Factors Which Improve the Sharing Process

Yet there are many things—*all* of which can be controlled by the sender and receiver—which can improve the prospects of true communications taking place. One of them, and the most basic, is the **message** itself. We instinctively pay greater attention to a sender who has an interesting and well-planned message. Despite the ability of the sender to deliver the message, *nothing substitutes for a good message. A speaker with good delivery who does not have a clear message offers his or her audience nothing more than a public performance of their acting ability.* Topic Choice will therefore be treated in Chapter Seven as the most important component of a good talk.

Another way to get the audience's attention is to *tell them to listen to you*, or to threaten them with action if they *don't* (like, show up for this class, or the instructor will give you a cut!). This is called **stimulation**, and it is effective in a limited sense—it gets the re-

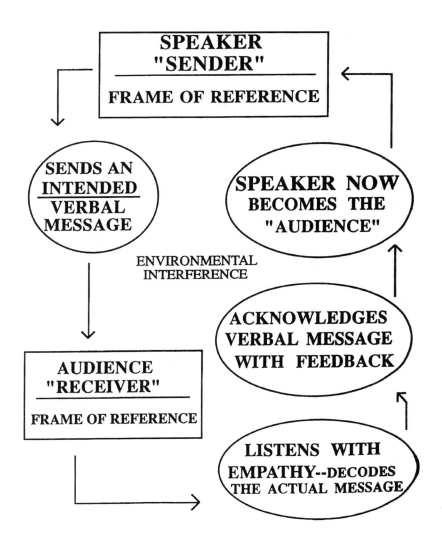

Figure 4.3

ceiver's initial attention, but once they're there, it's up to the sender to *keep* that attention. That's done with a number of strategies—a good sincere delivery, a message with a clarity of purpose—all of which will make an audience *want* to listen to you. This is an art, one that this course will concentrate on; the ability not to merely stimulate your audience, but to ***motivate*** them as well.

"Sharing" in Public

It's not you against them—it's you sharing with them. If you lose sight of this theoretical point, shown in our final diagram (see Figure 4.4), now a complete representation of the speech communications process, you will never fully master the art of public speaking. You don't stand in front of them and simply read a speech to them. You have to truly care about your message, so that the audience can too. You have to look at them, and they have to look at you. You have to negate as much "noise" as you can, and make your audience feel comfortable about coping with the interference that remains.

Think of it as the difference between ***"speeching" and "speaking."*** This book is designed to help you learn how to improve your ability to ***speak***—to communicate in public. We'll leave the "speeching" to the beginners and the phonies.

Hints to Remember

- Communications involves a sharing between a sender and receiver.

- With this thought in mind, the student of effective speaking will develop the technique of "speaking," rather than "speeching," to their audience.

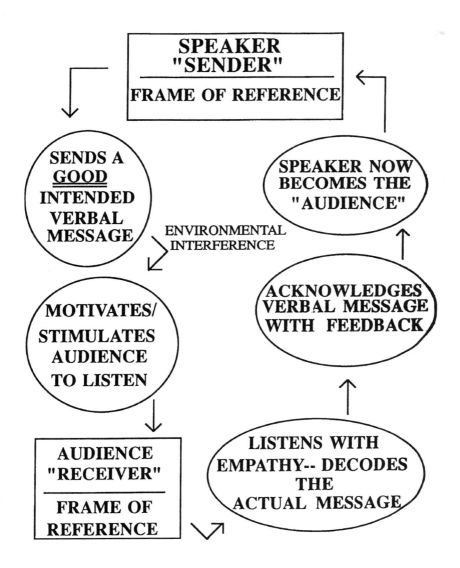

Figure 4.4

CHAPTER 5

On Having an Open Mind

Listening

What is a chapter about listening doing in a textbook about effective speaking? Maybe it would help to think back to the speech communication model discussed in the previous chapter. Speech communication, as we've seen, is a *process*. And as a process, it can only succeed if all aspects of the system are functioning well. Imagine that you have an engagement to deliver a speech in front of a large audience. You enter the auditorium, find the setting attractive, the lighting good, the podium in place. Your notes are well prepared, the stage is set, you are well rehearsed. As you stride to the front of the room, you notice an unexpected timbre in the voices of the audience members. You are about to deliver a speech to an audience of French men and women. And you know not a word of French! No matter how brilliant you are, it's very unlikely that they well be able to listen to you effectively. One of the very first steps, then, in preparing a speech is to understand the crucial importance of listening.

One of the common myths about effective listening is that is natural, like breathing, so we need to neither study it nor practice it. It's true, of course, that we *listen* all the time—far more than we read, write or speak. By some estimates, we spend more than 50% of our time listening.*

Poor listening habits can be very costly. If a supervisor has to repeat directions to an employee, that repetition costs time—and money. Poor listening on the part of employers or supervisors may result in neglect of important problems, sometimes until they reach

---

* e.g. Rudolph Vanderber and Ann Elder.

the crisis stage. Poor listening can result in canceled contracts and missed opportunities.

Causes of Poor Listening

- **Bias against the subject.** Have you already made up your mind on this topic? Do you find yourself thinking "We tried this before and it didn't work?"

- **Bias against the speaker.** Do you find it hard to listen to someone who is very attractive? Very unattractive? Of the opposite sex? Who is your subordinate?

- **External noise.** Is the room too noisy? Is there a hum from the lights that drives you crazy? Are the people behind you whispering?

- **Internal noise.** Are you distracted by personal problems? Worried about the speech *you* have to make in twenty minutes?

- **Mental 'spare time'.** Are you drifting off into imaginary worlds in between the speaker's phrases? This is related to the gap between thinking speed and speaking rate.

- **Poor listening habits.** Do you listen only for facts? Do you daydream? Do you pay more attention to the other members of the audience than you do to the speaker?

- **Inattention.** Do you fake it?

Strategies to Improve Your Listening

- **Learn to be an *active listener*.** Listen for cues within the speaker's presentation. Anticipate the points you think he or she will make. Summarize the main points as you go along. Take notes—but of main ideas, *not* word for word.

- **Prepare to listen.** Orient yourself to the speaking situation—for a class, come with the material read and thought about. For a lecture, find out about the speaker, the topic and the purpose *before you arrive.*

- **Distance yourself from your biases.** *If you don't open your mind, you'll never learn anything.* Listen to the speaker's message, try to understand his or his viewpoint, then refute it if you still disagree. At a minimum, you will have gained valuable insights into your opponent's views.

- **Avoid judging the message by evaluating the competence, appearance or delivery style of the speaker.** The audience who listened to Lincoln's "Gettysburg Address" felt the speech to be mediocre at best. History has given us a rather different evaluation.

- **Anticipate distractions in the environment and avoid them as much as possible.** Arrive early, prepared to change your location in the room if necessary. If you tend to get cold, bring a sweater. If the room tends to be overheated, dress in peel-off layers. If the sights outdoors tend to draw your attention, don't sit next to a window. Place yourself, if possible, in the front of the room, where you can see the speaker easily and hear him or her clearly.

- **Anticipate causes of internal noises and take steps to minimize them.** Don't go to a lecture hungry, hung over, or over-tired. Try to forget about the fight you've had with your boyfriend until after the class or lecture is over.

- **Recognize and use your mental 'spare time'.** If you are inclined to drift off, try instead to focus your concentration by asking yourself (and the speaker) questions in your mind. Why has he used a specific piece of evidence? Will she clarify her definition, or will you need to ask about it at the end of the lecture? Again, notetaking is useful here.

Remember that while, as noted in Chapters Two and Four, the speaker is in control of the speaking situation, you become an active part of the speaking process by providing the speaker with feedback. *It is not the speaker's job alone to "saw open your brain and pour it in."*

Hints to Remember

- Listening is hard work—you have to prepare for it just as you do for speaking.

- Don't judge the message by the speaker.

- Open your mind.

CHAPTER 6

An Asset, Not a Liability

Fear

_____

If you are afraid of public speaking, take heart in the fact that you are not alone. In a survey where people were asked to list their ten worst fears, public speaking was number one, ahead of death, financial ruin, spiders, and snakes.* The reasons for stage fright are numerous; some logical, some not. Most are interrelated. They all, however, contribute to one of the most common fears today.

Preparation is the Key

Every speaking experience presents an adventure into uncharted territory. Until your speech is completed, you cannot accurately know how you will come across. While you can predict situations, you can't accurately predict every variable. The key to counteracting the fear of the unknown is *preparation*. With proper preparation, you can easily make appropriate adaptations in your presentation.

Stage fright can be caused by the failure to address three major variables:

1. What constitutes a good speech
2. What your audience expects
3. A game plan to achieve 1 and 2.

A lack of preparation creates a *needless* foray into the unknown, thus increasing your risk of failure. The speaker who doesn't understand the mechanics of a good speech will not know if he or she is communicating effectively. A speaker who fails to assess the needs

---

* Christina Stuart, *Effective Speaking* (New York: Nichols Publishing, 1988), p. 72.

of the audience cannot effectively talk to them. Without a game plan, the speaker might as well speak in an impromptu mode—and improvise.[*] *Poor preparation, then, is the most common reason for stage fright.* It is also *easy to cure*, by using a simple combination of research and practice.

Overcoming Stage Fright

Even *with* good preparation, however, you will still be nervous. However, it need not control you. There are several ways to lower this stage fright to manageable levels.

- **Put the Speech in Perspective.** Remember, failure will rarely result in global destruction. Likewise, success will rarely make you president. Accept each speech as a *challenge*; an opportunity to learn and succeed. Relish the opportunity to convey your thoughts and to learn. If you perceive every chance to speak as a learning experience—*a personal challenge*—you will grow intellectually and personally.

- **Research Your Audience.** See our comments in Chapter Four.

- **Choose *Your* Topic and Prepare *Your* Speech.** See Our Comments in Chapters Seven through Ten (!).

- **Practice.** After you have prepared your basic outline and speaking notes, *rehearse it.* Use the mirror to give you a listener's perspective; rehearse in front of a professional who can give you worthwhile advice. Watch your mannerisms and correct those which will detract from your performance. Rehearsing your speech gives you the opportunity to "clean up" the rough spots, enabling you to make a better presentation. This will lessen your nerves.

- **Picture Success.** *Every speech is an opportunity to excel.* Visualize your success. Rather than fearing potential failure, anticipate positive outcomes. Use the speech as a

---

[*] Abne M. Eisenberg, *Painless Public Speaking* (New York: Macmillan Publishing, 1982), p. 163. See Chapter Eighteen of this book for more on Impromptu Speaking.

motivator. If you think optimistically, your chances of success improve.

Emotion—be it fear, anxiety, apprehension, excitement, or anticipation—*is an absolute necessity in public speaking.* While combating stage fright is desirable, eliminating it causes an equally undesirable effect: **boredom.** Stage fright is the body's way of communicating excitement. If you are excited, you will communicate in a superior fashion. However, public speaking is a risk; yet without risk, there is no return. Use stage fright as a motivator to excel. Harness it. Properly channelled, it can be the difference between mediocrity and success.

Hints to Remember

- Preparation lessens fear.
- Accept each speech as a challenge to succeed, rather than as an opportunity to fail.
- Fear will *never* disappear. That's *good*, because you can use it to your advantage.

CHAPTER 7

Mission Possible

Choosing and Researching Your Topic

By now you might be thinking: *I can't choose a topic.* I don't have any ideas. I can't think of anything to write. Sound familiar? Our advice: Don't think, write. Whether you are searching for an idea for a writing assignment or for a speech, *you have to write to think.*

Your Topic As *You*

To get started, get pen in hand and write for ten minutes without stopping. Have someone time you, or use a timer. By freewriting, your mind will become more lucid and many ideas will surface. For all you thinkers who don't think you have anything to write, try it. Circle all of the ideas you wrote on about two pages, then list them on a separate sheet of paper. Some students prefer to cluster or map their ideas, but try at least one of these. Whatever you choose, document the ideas you come up with, no matter how ridiculous they seem to you. One idea triggers another idea.

Start with yourself. *You are the topic.* You are the best source for materials. You have a wealth of different experiences you have lived through. Some of you have lived in more than one place and had to change schools. You all have various family traditions and special holiday memories. You also have your "firsts". Think back to your earliest memory, and then proceed chronologically. For instance, what *is* your earliest memory? Where were you? Who was with you? At this period of your life, list the members of your family, and where you lived, and certain things that will help you recall that particular time of your life.

Keep going . . . think back to your first day of school. Let yourself be a kindergartner again, and let those feelings of excitement, loneliness, and bewilderment come back. List people who were there: your teacher, your best friend, and other friends, and list things you did. Then list the first pet you remember, your first bike, your first boyfriend or girlfriend, your first kiss, your first day in middle school, your first day in high school, your first date, your first driving lesson, and so on. When you run out of firsts, you might want to list *favorites*. For instance: your favorite toy, your favorite stuffed animal, your favorite relative, your favorite vacation, and so on.

Some people like to start with their most *recent* experience. For example, if you are a college freshman or sophomore, list memories from your first day at college. Then describe your high school graduation, and continue in this fashion to your first memory. When you either finish or take a break from this activity, you'll find that your subconscious will still be at work, conjuring up things you hadn't thought about for a long time. You will want, therefore, to take along a note pad with you so you can jot these things down as they come to you.

Another way to brainstorm topics is to take a *personal inventory* of things you've done, hobbies you enjoy, awards or honors you've received, sports you like to participate in or watch, and other interests. *Look at your resume.* It should help, since it contains your special skills and talents, accomplishments, and previous occupations.

The key to any topic is that you pick something that you already have some knowledge of, and one you are truly sincere and enthusiastic about. Then, because you're excited, you will want to learn more about this topic and research it more fully. When you finally deliver your speech, your sincerity and enthusiasm will be contagious and spread to your audience.

It should be obvious to you that *you need to plan ahead*. Speech preparation requires thought, creativity, research, and organization. When you get to this point, you, the speechwriter, need a mental break. Then you're ready to start writing the speech, which is covered in the next chapter.

Hints to Remember

- The best topics come from your personal experience.

- All good speakers are audience-centered. Adapt your research to meet your audience's particular needs and interests.

- Care about your topic and about your audience.

CHAPTER 8

Blueprints

Outlining the Body

You've chosen your topic. Now comes the hard part: writing the speech. Imagine yourself a draftsperson, and you're sitting at your drafting table. *Your task is to draw a blueprint of your speech.*

The General Purpose

The general purpose statement is *simply the purpose of the speech with the infinitive "to" before the verb.* For example, if your purpose is to inform the audience of something, then the general purpose statement is to inform. What are the general purposes for giving speeches? To name a few: to inform, to persuade, to entertain, to inspire, to stimulate, to introduce, and to create good will.

The Exact Purpose

The second step helps you, as the writer of your speech, focus on the thesis of your talk. The exact purpose is analogous to the thesis statement in a written composition. It has to be specific, precise, and to the point. Like all good writing, and ultimately, speaking, *you need to state specifically what your speech is about and what you intend to accomplish.*

The exact purpose statement should also be preceded by the verb "to." Word choice is important here because your language needs to be clear so the audience knows *exactly* what your speech is all about, and where you are headed (for example: "Today I would like to teach you about the importance of retention and review as a study skill"). At this early stage, you have to orient them and prepare them mentally so they can follow your course of action. Limit your statement to *one major idea* and make sure you can achieve your objective in the time allotted.

Main Idea

Your statement of exact purpose is always found in the introduction of your speech. The main idea is found in the body of your speech. *It is the message or the idea you want your listeners to go away with.* The main idea is written entirely from the listener's point-of-view, whereas the statement of exact purpose is written from *your* point-of-view.

Let's create an informative talk on the above mentioned topic—on using recitation and review as a study skill. So far, your blueprint looks like this:

Statement of General Purpose: To inform.

Statement of Exact Purpose: To inform you of the importance of recitation and review as a study skill.

Statement of Main Idea: The use of recitation and review will improve your test scores.

The Body of the Talk

The body of your speech comes next. It is by far the most voluminous section of your speech. The main points organized in the body of your speech will *explain your main idea;* your support will help prove it (see the next chapter on this point). Don't overload with main ideas. Keep it two or three main points—*your main points are the main ideas found in your main idea.*

For our sample talk, your main idea is that recitation and review, if used properly, will increase your test scores. To get to your main points, start with recitation: *why* recitation? Explain first what you mean by recitation, then discuss the research you found that backs up this assertion. Then move to the *next* **main point** found in your central idea—review—and do the same as you did for your first main point.

Your blueprint will now look something like this:

Statement of General Purpose: To inform.

Statement of Exact Purpose: To inform you of the importance of recitation and review as a study skill.

Statement of Main Idea: The use of recitation and review will improve your test scores.

BODY

I. Main Point: Recitation will improve test scores

    A.   Definition of recitation

        1.   Example

II. Main Point: Review

    A.   Review will improve test scores

        1.   Support: Research Findings & More Statistics

    B.   More Information on Review

        1.   When to Review
        2.   Support: Example

Transitions

Writers supply transitions when there is a shift in thought, such as the introduction of a new idea. Transitions are signals that a change, shift, or new material is coming up; or an example, comparison, or some support material is to follow. *They help you go from one point to the next.* Just as in any writing, in speech making, you need to cue your listeners.

Here are just some of many transitional words and phrases to choose from:

Purpose	Word or Phrase
To show addition	also, and, and then, as well, for one thing, furthermore, in addition, moreover.
to show comparison	both, in the same way, likewise, similarly
to show contrast	although, but, even though, however, in contrast, on the other hand
to show emphasis	especially, in particular, most importantly
to show an example, an illustration	a case in point, another example of, another instance of, as an illustration, for example, for instance
to show conclusion, summary	all in all, finally, on the whole, to sum up

The Speaking Outline

Outlines help the speaker include main points, details for support materials, and organize the points in a logical sequence. The speaking outline is different than those you've written for writing courses. *Your speaking outline will be longer.* This outline is usually written in *complete sentences,* with transitions supplied between the introduction and body, between the main points, and the body and the conclusion.

You might find after you have written your outline that you need to *edit.* You should *time your speech* and determine if it is too long or too short. If it is too long, delete the most unimportant support material, and if it is too short you should add more support. Now you're ready to support this outline with your researched support material.

Hints to Remember

- Whatever format you use for outlining, keep it consistent.

CHAPTER 9

Support Yourself

Research and Support Material

Why should we, your audience, *believe* what you are telling us? What *proof* do you have to back-up what you are saying? Your audience expects respect from you; part of that respect comes from the evidence that you offer to your audience as proof of your claims. This evidence, or support material, can come from the library, from interviews, or from surveys. When this material is prepared for use in your talk, it can take five general forms: testimony, examples (including narratives), facts, statistics, and definitions.

The Library

After you choose a topic, go to the library to start your search for support materials. Re-acquaint yourself with the layout of your library and its sources. Explore the subject card catalog to see what information is available on a given topic. Roam the aisles in the periodical section and look for new ideas in magazines and journals in your field of interest. Search the vertical files for more up-to-date statistics and findings on controversial topics. Another area worth investigating is, of course, the reference section where you will find books useful to speechwriters. For instance, you will find Bartlett's *Familiar Quotations* and *Unfamiliar Quotations*, *Dictionary of Questions*, and *The World's Greatest Speeches*, to name a few. There are journals that deal with the communication process, speech writing, and speech delivery, such as *Journal of Communication* and *Vital Speeches*. If you can't find what you are looking for in your library, ask your librarian about an interlibrary loan policy. Most colleges and universities can acquire materials from other such institutions in their area. Think, too, of visual aids you will be using in the upcoming speeches, because you might find something you can use in the library (see Chapter Fifteen). For instance, there is usually a section of folio books that have vivid photographs and art work contained within.

The Informative Interview and The Survey

You might want to think about interviewing someone who is knowledgeable in the field you're interested in talking about. Don't be reluctant to ask someone for an interview; most people are flattered when you ask them for an interview, and will be delighted to give you a little of their time. Interviews are an excellent source for obtaining an interesting narrative or funny anecdote for your speech.

There are two kinds of interviews: *phone* interviews for people who are too far away, and *person-to-person* interviews. If you need a phone number, by the way, look for an 800 directory in your library. It contains a listing of most agencies, corporations, and the like. If you are going to conduct the interview over the phone there is a certain etiquette you must adhere to. Choose a convenient time for the interviewee, and get an idea ahead of time of their time limitations. If you plan on tape recording the interview, you must get the interviewee's permission beforehand. Even if you are recording the interview, you should take good notes in case of mechanical breakdown. Prepare questions in advance and try to find out something about the person you are going to interview. Ask your prepared questions and get as much background and information as possible. Immediately after the interview, rewrite your notes so you can fill-in the gaps and elaborate while it's still fresh in your head. Take time to write a short thank you note to your interviewee.

For the person-to-person interview, you need to call ahead of time to make an appointment. Again, before the interview do some research to give yourself adequate background on your interviewee. You'll want to prepare questions as with any interview, but ask questions that require full-bodied responses, not 'yes' or 'no' answers. When you meet with your interviewee start in a relaxed friendly way, but keep things professional. Thank them for their time and exchange a few quick pleasantries. *Try to get as much information as possible*; remember, this is the time you might get a humorous story or unusual fact about your speech topic. Look over your prepared questions before you leave the interview to see if you omitted anything. This, in most instances, will be your last chance to ask questions. Repeat anything that you are not sure of. As with your phone interview, interview go over your notes, and redo them if necessary, and send a thank you note for your interviewee's time.

Besides interviews, you can conduct public opinion polls by taking a *survey*. Whether your samples are random or select, ask each group the *same set of questions* for validity and for the sake of consistency. Another way to gather information is to personally investigate a place or a group of people. For instance, if your topic deals with child abuse, you might want to get in touch with Catholic Charities or some other agency in your area. Refer to the yellow pages for possibilities. Don't forget to check a nearby video store; you may find more information on video tape or film.

Forms of Presenting Support Material

Now let's look at five of the ways that you can *present* this research material to your audience.

When a person uses **testimony,** he or she is telling the audience what another person (hopefully, an authority) has said on the subject. Testimony can be in the form of a quote, in which the authority's comments are given word-for-word, or testimony can be given as paraphrase. Here, the authority's comments are put in the speaker's own words (thus, it is *perfect* for your interview material!).

Avoid plagiarism (stealing another person's ideas); **whether you are quoting, paraphrasing, or passing on other forms of support, tell the audience who the source of the information is.**

Examples are specific instances that demonstrate an idea. They help us to visualize what you are saying; they help us to understand. **Narratives** are examples in story form (preferably *short*) which highlight or demonstrate an idea. A narrative can be from the author's experience or from that of a third party. They add life to a speech, and they can be used as attention-getters.

Facts are among this planet's most elusive creatures. We tend to endow facts with benevolent and almost god-like qualities. An idea on which we bestow the title "fact" instantly achieves undeniable credibility; it *must* be true . . .

Oh?

Let's define "fact" as *verifiable information*. If information is verifiable, it can be shown to be true . . . or false. From this definition, we can draw three conclusions about this critter:

- **First, a fact deals with the *past or the present*.** It cannot deal with the future. (How can you prove the statement? The incident in question has not happened yet!)

- **Second, facts *change*.** Records of events and ideas change as documents—private, business, and government—have been found to have "false facts" (either by mistake or by design). And here we reach our third conclusion regarding the almighty fact:

- **Facts can be *false*.**

Another form of support, **statistics**, are facts which use numbers to measure things. They should be stated as complete thoughts. "1994" is not a statistic. "My mailbox number is 1994" also does not qualify. "There are 1,994 square feet in this hall" is, yes, a statistic.

One member of the statistics family, the *average*, has evolved into three different forms. Mean, median, and mode averages lurk everywhere. We usually assume that an 'average' refers to the mean (such as a college Grade Point Average, or GPA), but that is not always the case. Speakers and authors might chose different types of averages to support their main idea. This error can lead to conflicting conclusions.

Definitions are the mites of language. We often give them little notice; they seem so small and insignificant that they are hardly worth investigating. Yet these little guys are responsible for our understanding of "truth," of what is. What is a "manager trainee" in this company? Does that individual stock the shelves, mop the floor, clean the toilets . . .? Or, does (s)he operate a cash register, take inventory, and collect hourly employees' time tickets? Or . . .

By providing your audience with a healthy amount of *quality* support material, you are helping to show your audience that you respect them, and, you are building your own credibility: we will be more inclined to believe—and respect—you.

Hints to Remember

- Support your support material by telling your listeners the source of that information.

- Use your knowledge of evidence to analyze the support material of other speakers; be a critical listener.

CHAPTER 10

Get Them Interested . . .
Leave Them Interested

The Introduction and Conclusion

Imagine a news magazine or a television documentary as a plateau. Each is a different place, of sorts, where your thoughts may have been before encountering that article or show. Usually, the creators of each message have provided you with a "slope" to gently bring you to the top of this plateau, where you will find the important information in the article or show, and a slope to bring you back to where you were when you began.

As a speaker, you want to provide your listener with the same kind of path into and out of your speech; in other words, you want to offer your listener with an introduction and a conclusion.

Your introduction and conclusion, then, serve three main purposes. They:

- **guide your listeners into and out of your speech,**

- **advise the audience about your topic and main idea, and**

- **let your audience know when your speech begins and ends.**

How do you do this?

First, *prepare the body of your talk.* Once you have polished your main idea, exact purpose statement, and your main points, then you have a clear idea of what you want your audience to know (your main idea may well change as you research and develop your information; if you prepare the introduction first, you may get us ready for information which is not in your speech). Also, once you have prepared the body of your speech, you know what you want to say, why you want to say it, who your audience is, and what response you want from that audience. Now, you can wrap your speech in an appropriate introduction and conclusion.

The Introduction

Your introduction serves a variety of roles. The first goal of your introduction is to *grab our attention*. You want to mentally whisk us away from the actual situation—the time and place of the speech—you want to beckon us, tempt us, seduce us into following your words. How? Your introductory information can imaginatively incorporate any number of qualities which generate interest, such as activity, familiarity, novelty, suspense, conflict, and "the vital" (things and/or ideas necessary for life).

How will you put these factors into words? Your answer rests largely in the support material discussed in the previous chapter—use examples, facts, statistics, narratives, or questions. The ways in which you can use these are unlimited; just be sure that your method is *appropriate for the audience, for the situation, and for the topic*. For example, the information should be understandable by—and not offensive to—your audience. A somber situation calls for matching introduction (and topic). Be sure that your introduction, including, and especially, your attention-grabber, are *relevant to the topic*.

A *brief story* which serves as an illustration of your main idea is an often-used method of introduction, especially a *real-life ("human-interest") story* which highlights the experience of a single individual of small group. Rather than being expressed as a fact which discusses a faceless multitude, an idea can more easily mesmerize us if it is represented through the gut-wrenching tale of a single individual with whom we can identify.

A *question* can also be put to work for you. If, for example, you will be discussing a certain part of the world or a certain event, you might ask audience members to raise their hands if they've been there. In doing so, you are generating activity on their part and you are raising a topic with which they are familiar. A *rhetorical question* is one for which you do not expect your audience to provide an answer; its purpose is to get them thinking. "When was the last time you volunteered to help your community?" is a rhetorical question that a speaker might use to begin a speech on the importance of volunteerism.

After grabbing our attention, your introduction provides you with an ideal opportunity in which to *explain the importance of your speech.* This is a continuation of the development of interest in the topic.At the same time, you also have a chance to *begin developing your credibility.* Clue us into your knowledge on the subject; start forming for yourself the image, the reputation, of an individual who is sincere, knowledgeable, trustworthy, and concerned for the audience.

Your introduction (especially in a informative speech) also serves to *tell us your main idea and to preview your main points.* In doing so, you tell us what kind of ideas to expect and what subtopics you will cover. This helps us listen for improved understanding and it helps us to remember the content of your talk. This may well involve giving your audience your *exact purpose statement.*

The Conclusion

Now, what should you keep in mind when designing your conclusion? Remember we mentioned that your conclusion needs to guide us on a return trip from the world discussed in your speech, and into the time and place we "left" when you began talking.

Your conclusion, therefore, should let us know that we have covered all the information of the speech, and that we are at the end. One way of doing this is to cover **only** the main points which you previewed in your introduction. Avoid adding more ideas; we would not be expecting more (and therefore different) information.

After you have made your final comment on your final point, vocal variety (perhaps in the form of a pause) can indicate to us that you have covered the promised information. At this point, you will begin leading us back from this metaphorical plateau. With skillful use of wording and vocal variety, you will be able to avoid uttering those dreaded two words: "In conclusion . . ." Droll! Boring!! Offensive!!!

As your guests on this journey, we would probably appreciate a "memento" of the experience. That souvenir could be a brief summary of your main points; it could also be a memorable (and, of course, relevant!) quote, rhetorical question, challenge, or (in a persuasive speech) call to action.

Your attention-grabber provides you with an additional option. *Plug us back into that attention-grabber*; it was the path we trekked along to enter the realm of your speech. By following it once more after discussing the promised main point, we realize that we are returning to where we started. Tell us *where* we can volunteer to help the community (for a persuasive speech in which you want us to behave in a certain way, ask us to volunteer at that place).

Each day, we can use the lessons learned during this chapter. How, for example, techniques we have discussed can be used in other message plateaus, such as reports, in letters home, and in daily conversation. You, as a writer/speaker, become a more understandable—and even a more *interesting* person.

Hints to Remember

- Prepare the *body* of your talk *first*, then create the introduction and conclusion.

- Be sure that your introduction and conclusion are relevant to, and appropriate for your audience, topic, and purpose.

- In an informative speech, use your introduction and conclusion to preview and review your central idea and main points.

- Link your attention-getter with your conclusion.

CHAPTER 11

Sketchy, Not Scripted

Speaking Notes

After you're done "writing" your talk—that is, putting your major points, supporting material, introduction, and conclusion down in sketchy, outline form—then it's time to think about your speaking notes.

No, your outline from Chapter Nine is **not** your speaking notes. If you did your outline correctly, then it should be a bit messy—with things crossed out, inserted—it should represent the *thinking* portion of speech writing. It is, hopefully, a sketchy "blueprint;" It is still, however, not "clean" enough to be taken to the podium. Also, there are probably some things that are **not** on your outline that *should* be on your speaking notes. If done correctly, your speaking notes will help your delivery—they will actually help your eye contact, vocal speed, and even your pacing!

First, a quick look at what these notes are *not*. They are *not*:

- **a full word-for-word manuscript.** We are not teaching Oral Reading here. We are teaching, as noted earlier, "speaking," not "speeching." Being chained to a speech which is written out word-for-word takes away your spontaneity, your ability to maintain eye contact, and your sincerity. You'll just sound like you're *"reading."* We are aiming for a skill that one national aptitude examination calls "speaking on your feet,"and what speech professionals call *extemporaneous speaking*—scripts make it *impossible* to learn this skill.

They are also *not*:

- <u>**No**</u> **Notes**. Trying to deliver a talk from memory runs many of the same risks as trying to read it verbatim. When you are worried about *remembering* what you've memorized, you're *not thinking about speaking to the audience.* And trust us—the one thing that is common to all speakers who try to speak from memory is that they *will* forget something—it's just a matter of how important a point they will forget, and how much more nervous it will make them when it happens.

Then what *are* these notes? One way to look at it is that they are a *cleaner version of your outline.* This does *not* mean that they are typed. In fact, that's not a great idea—imagine trying to **see** this printed page, some three to four feet away from you, while you're nervous. The notes should be *written in a heavy, black/blue marker or pen*, and, for best results for seeing them while trying to speak at the same time, *printed, not cursively written.*

Most important, however, is the **amount** of material that you include in your notes. For beginning speakers, the next few hints are, perhaps, the most nerve-wracking that you will find in this book, because we are simply *not* in favor of writing out full ideas on your notes. If you already know a great deal about your topic, you won't have to—you'll only need a word or two—a sentence at most, for a statistic, direct quote, or some other piece of supporting evidence—that will jog your memory about the point you wish to tell us. *Your notes should include only that material which will remind you of the point that you are trying to share, not the entire point written out word-for-word.* <u>*They should include nothing more.*</u>

Thinking about this point for the first time, your reaction would be very normal if it went something like: "No **way**. I can't get up there with only a few words—I'll forget my whole talk, and look like an incoherent idiot." *Only if you didn't pay attention to our chapter on topic choice.* If you didn't choose a topic that you already know something about (credibility), and care deeply about (sincerity), then all the words in the world won't help. But if your topic *was* chosen after giving it this kind of thought, then *all you will **need** is a word or two to jog your memory.* Without having a full script, you'll be able to glance at the podium, remind yourself of the next point, look at us, and talk to us (the trick is not, incidentally, to pretend that the notes aren't there—if that was the case, we'd have you memorize it! Glance at the notes, then look at the audience . . .). We'll be talking about the value of *body movement* in Chapter Fourteen—breaking the plane of the podium, and walking out tho the front to talk with us. How can *that* be done if you're chained to either a lengthy script, or a faulty memory? And, to carry the point one step further—if we are more prone to *listen* to someone who has good physical delivery, we are certainly more prone to *listen* to a person who isn't reading word-for-word, or stumbling over a poorly memorized talk.

Oh . . . after all this on keeping it sketchy, there's one thing that you'll want to *add*. Speaking professionals call them **"cues."** They consist of a word or two to help you to deal with any delivery problem that you might have. For example—in **red ink**, so that they stand out—"LOOK UP!" "SLOW DOWN!" "RELAX!" Granted, these don't work all the time, but they don't get in the way of the speaker, and they may well give you the reminder that you need to improve yourself while being at the podium.

Perhaps the biggest question that arises from this entire discussion—*how much is too much?*

Would **"Your Guess Is As Good as Mine"** be too flip an answer to include in a textbook? Because that's really the answer. Whether or not you have included too much on your notes is something that you and your instructor will have to discuss after your first talk. It is difficult to proclaim "rules" here. It depends on how long your talk must be, how big or small you write, the requirements of a particular instructor, and your own self-confidence level. But let us reiterate; there is no rule more important to the development of good notecards than this one:

Hints to Remember

- The less on your notes, the better.

CHAPTER 12

A Change of Sound

Oral Delivery

Oral delivery is a touchy subject. It seems we can apply outside research and rational thought when we compose and arrange *ideas* for our speeches, but we were *born* with our voices. Vocal expressiveness is a factor of personality.

Many students begin effective speaking classes resigned to the viewpoint that 'their voices are their voices,' and there is no turning back. But think about it. As one writer put it so well, have some of us committed "voice suicide," living with a "tired voice"?[*] Think about the vocal range of a child or a young teenager telling a story. Lots of emotion and enthusiasm there. If we were once those kids, what's happened since?

We need not accept this "tired voice" as our speaking voice—we *can* effect some positive change. It's possible to learn voice control, although that takes some rather tedious vocal coaching. On a more general level, it certainly is possible for anyone in an effective speaking class to improve pitch and tone on their phrasing, and to choose words that will give a voice more vibrancy. Here are just a few pointers for a crash course:

Testing, 1, 2, 3. . . .

You will have to record your voice on audio tape if you're serious about making some changes. Record all of your speeches to groups, from beginning to end. Also, record some conversations with friends. Do some exercises on the tape recorder as well—repeat

---

[*] Morton Cooper, "Don't Put Up With Voice Fatigue," *Wall Street Journal*, September 28, 1992, p. A12.

phrases like "Fleet Street is Neat," pronounce every "T," *and* say it with five different emotions. Recite poetry, news articles—any set of phrases to help you out.

Tone/Pitch

For our purposes, *tone and pitch* can be used interchangeably. Caused by the frequency in the vibration of the vocal cords, they convey the expressiveness in your emotions. When you are surprised and you squeal "What!!!", followed up by a much lower, indignant "You're *kidding!*", you are employing a change in pitch or tone to make your feelings known. It's not necessarily louder or softer than your usual words, so don't mistake it for volume when you practice.

One of the reasons students seem to find their tone and pitch so difficult to vary is because they think that a speech is terribly different from the tone of conversation, and that they should try to sound 'scholarly and formal.' Pam Zarit, a media trainer and president of her own communications company in New York, cautions against this formal tone, adding that people should "try to make themselves sound approachable and *real* by letting their natural speech patterns come through."[*]

So, our best advice here is to *consciously listen to yourself* when you're explaining ideas to people on an everyday basis, and notice what you like about your vocal delivery, so that you can keep some of that tone for your speeches. Again, the tape recorder will help you here. You must try to sound as conversational as possible (the quality that many professionals call *"conversational tone"*). Be especially conscious of changing the 'up and down' sound of certain words. You can vary the sounds of words by remembering that your voice *needs* enthusiasm and feeling. Some students think they'll be considered foolish if they put any feeling into their speeches. Not so. Experience in our own classes indicates that student audiences are always extremely receptive to the speaker who puts some sincere "oomph" into his or her words.

---

[*]   Pam Zarit, "Public Speaking Survival Strategies," *Working Woman*, November, 1990, p. 120.

Volume

Many students speak too softly when they first speak before a group. This is usually due to lack of speaking experience, as well as a lack of confidence. In our everyday conversation, we speak to people who are about two feet away from us. For a presentation, our voices have to project over a classroom or a lecture hall with the listeners situated in a sound arc that extends before us as well as to the left and right.

To improve your volume, rehearse speeches while you're at one end of a room and your listeners are at the other end. Keep your head *up*, so the sound can come from your mouth in an imaginary line that's level with the heads in the audience. Don't speak up *unnaturally*: you shouldn't have to strain your throat, because it's actually the interaction of your tongue and lips *with* the throat that will aid your volume.[*] Also, don't open your mouth very wide, thinking that a wider mouth automatically emits a louder sound. You'll just look funny, and you'll make your jaw tired.

Pronounciation

Without clear, correct pronounciation, *nothing else in a speech matters very much*. Listeners may put up with a less-than-animated oral delivery, but they'll surrender quickly if they don't understand what you're saying.

Clear, correct pronounciation involves three efforts: familiarity with a variety of words, a conscious attempt to say *every* part of a word, and a speaking rate that's slow enough so that the endings of words don't blur into the beginnings of the next word. Listen to newscasters and special TV commentaries to broaden your speaking vocabulary and to hear the pronounciation of words you may have only read in print. Newscasters can also be good models for clear pronounciation (if you don't copy their stilted, punch-like manner of delivery). Slowing down contributes considerably to clearer pronounciation.

You should be aware of some common problems in pronounciation, and practice to avoid them. For instance, *people often let their*

---

[*] Ralph Proodian, "Mind the Tip of Your Tongue," *Wall Street Journal,* May 4, 1992, p. A16.

last syllables die by allowing their voices to trail off. Closings, whether their last words or last syllables, should have some impact. *Don't lower and soften your voice at the end of a sentence.* Rehearse difficult long words—*like "meteorology"*—separately, then rehearse them within a sentence, especially within your central idea.

Pauses

Silence—in the right amount and in the right places—is as powerful as the right word.

Pauses are very important for emphasis. You can control an audience's receptiveness to a word or an idea if you pause long enough, *with eye contact,* for them to know that the word is important. You should also pause before and after a transition statement.

In order to know precisely when to pause, you have to know what ideas are important to you, so that you can stop *naturally* when you care enough to do so. You also have to know which key words and concepts you want your listeners to take home with them. Those are the words and concepts you must give some time to. And remember that your *eye contact must accompany any pause*, so that the audience knows you're stopping *deliberately*.

Oral delivery *is* an extension of the person inside of you. You can reveal that person by being aware of the vocal techniques in this chapter. Remember that underlying all these techniques is *your concern for having your message heard and remembered.* In front of a group, *you are a voice*, so make it your best voice, in your best conversational tone.

Hints to Remember

- You *must* vary the quality and volume of your vocal delivery.

- Listening to yourself in everyday speaking situations will help you to do this.

CHAPTER 13

Made Ya Look

Physical Delivery: Eye Contact

Let's say you were preparing for a career on the stage. You would be instructed *never* to make real eye contact with the audience. The reason? Making eye contact with the audience shatters the illusion that you are Hamlet or Ophelia. Instead, it makes you a "real" person—an actor or actress playing a part.

For that very reason, in public speaking, you *always* make eye contact—because it makes you a real person to your audience, and it makes your audience real people to you. That's a very good place to start when you are trying to communicate.

Don't Make Me Look . . .

Of course, if you've got a major case of stage fright, it might seem comforting to imagine there is not a single person in the audience. Once you make eye contact, however, you are most likely to be in for a pleasant surprise. *Feedback is your most immediate payback for making eye contact.*

"Hold it," you say. "How do I know the feedback is going to be positive? What if the audience is sitting there sneering at me?"

Well, there are no guarantees. But, unless you are speaking at *The Rocky Horror Picture Show*, your audience is unlikely to throw things. In fact, in most speaking situations, *the audience starts off on your side.* To *keep* them on your side, you have to establish that eye contact early.

Eye contact allows you begin to 'read' your audience—to detect when they are with you and when they are not. That gives you the opportunity to adjust your speech or your delivery style in response

49

to the audience. If your audience looks bewildered, you can back up and clarify the parts that were baffling. If the audience seems bored, you might ask them if the material is already familiar to them, so that you can move ahead. Or, perhaps their boredom is due to physical conditions like an overheated room. This "noise" (remember Chapter Four?) can be remedied simply by opening a window. The point is, if you don't know that a problem exists—and it's hard to know without making eye contact—then you can't fix the problem.

There is, too, that magical kind of feedback that we always want to get—again received when we make eye contact—that shows that the audience is spellbound by your speech. That kind of feedback raises your performance level still higher and makes for the most successful public speaking. But, it is that feedback that you will never know unless you make eye contact.

How to Look

By now, you should be thoroughly convinced that eye contact is an important element in public speaking. But, what does making eye contact really mean? Certainly, you wouldn't want to try to stare down the audience. What eye contact means, in the public speaking arena, is the frequent look to many members of the audience that nonverbally says, "Are you with me?" or "I am enjoying sharing this with you!" or "How am I doing?" The look may last for only a few seconds—long enough for you to ask a question or make a comment with your eyes—and long enough to get a nonverbal reply from the members of the audience you have established eye contact with.

Here are additional ground rules for making good eye contact.

- **Rehearse**. Yes, we're back to that. It stands to reason that if you are not well rehearsed, your eyes will be glued to your speaking notes and you won't dare make eye contact with the audience for fear of losing your place. Rehearse that speech until you are comfortable enough to really look at your audience.

- **Remind Yourself.** If you have a tendency to not look at your audience, write cues in your speaking notes, as suggested in Chapter Eleven. But, *be careful!* Too often we see speakers who do the obligatory and all too mechanical "Look at the Audience" as reminded by their speaking notes. That doesn't count. Nor does lifting your head and giving your audience a frozen stare. You really have to make eye contact.

- **Look at *All* of Your Audience.** That doesn't mean that you have to make eye contact with every person in the audience. It does mean that you should make eye contact with people in the front and toward the back of the audience, and to the right and left of you. If you only look at your best friend sitting in the front row center, the rest of your audience will soon feel left out, and quite curious as to exactly who it is you are looking at. To keep them interested in you and in what you are saying, look around.

- **Know where *not* to look.** Staring intently at the ceiling, out of the window, or at the floor is a sure way of taking your audience's mind off of your speech. Human nature dictates that the audience looks where the speaker is looking. Your eyes cast upward do not cause your audience to think of you as thoughtful so much as they make your audience wonder what is on the ceiling. Look at your audience, look at your notes, and don't look anywhere else.

If your mother ever told you, "Look at me when I'm talking to you!", then you received early lessons in the importance of eye contact—whether you are the speaker or the listener. Practice the techniques suggested in this chapter to polish your eye contact skills.

Hints to Remember

- Eye contact builds a bridge over which communication can travel.

- Look at audience members in many different parts of the room.

- Establish eye contact early in your speech.

- Use eye contact to 'read' feedback from your audience.

CHAPTER 14

Move.

Physical Delivery: The Case for Movement

As members of an audience who've watched lengthy presentations for years in school, you are probably quite able to evaluate physical delivery. Which teacher or professor did you find more interesting: the person who stood up at the blackboard or lectern for the entire period and got *through* the material without looking for reactions from the class? Or was it the person who moved *into* the aisle, changed locations around the room, and came up to you and looked you in the eye? Chances are that the latter instructor was more sensitive to his or her students, and more apt to adjust phrasing and vocal expressiveness. True, you sometimes found all that activity discomfiting—"Am I going to be put on the spot here?"—but you *didn't* fall asleep, and you *did* listen.

Move. It's the single best piece of advice we can give to people who want to improve their physical delivery. In particular, *abandoning the lectern* could be the single most helpful behavior you could cultivate. By changing location from the front of the room and moving closer to the audience, you will find that other important speaking behaviors fall into place. Your voice sounds louder and more clear. You make eye contact more naturally. Your listeners tend to watch you more closely, so their interest buoys your confidence and you continue speaking strongly. And you establish rapport because you appear more sincere and personable—*closer is friendlier.*

Bert Decker, a documentary filmmaker who now teaches a course on communicating to business executives, considers the lectern off-limits. Forbidding the lectern's use underlies his larger consideration—that you as a speaker have "to reach people emotionally, not mechanically, if you want to cause change."[*] A talking head at a lectern can be rather mechanical. And if the audience appears indifferent to the message delivered by such a speaker, then the speaker feels more tension and delivers less "oomph."

So *why* do you want to stand up there, in the front, all by yourself, with a piece of furniture? If you're like most of our students, you like the lectern for three reasons: it's a place to prop up your speaking notes, it's a place to rest your hands, and it hides most of your body so you don't feel stared at.

We can tell you to use your hands, and stop being self-conscious about people watching you. But we know from our own experiences, and those of our students, that you don't change into a brilliant orator just by reading a few rules. You are not going to begin your first presentation by throwing yourself into the aisle, and then being able to maintain rapport by gazing sincerely at every face you see. Nor *should* you.

We suggest small trials. For example: step in front of the lectern *once*, while you're showing a photo or chart. You'll see the favorable effect your movement makes on the audience.

Here are some common fears surrounding physical movement which we have heard from our students, and our suggestions for circumventing those fears. These are *real* solutions to your fears, not *ideal* ones. The aim here is to control your physical delivery by consciously adding variety and naturalness to your movements. Ideally, confidence will follow.

1. I can't leave the lectern because my notecards are there, and I'll forget everything I wanted to say.

Suggestions:

- Make your speaking notes on the smallest index cards possible, and *take them with you*. Be familiar with the material so that you aren't looking down at the cards all the time. Even with the cards in your hands, the audience will enjoy your message if you're closer.

---

[*] Dick Janssen, "Putting More Oomph in Your Oratory," *Business Week*, June 4, 1990, p. 165.

- Use the overhead projector and put up a transparency on which you've phrased your main points or topics. Keep it on the screen throughout your presentation, and wander from location to location, referring to your main points as reminders of what you want to say next.

2. I tried standing away from the lectern, and my mind went blank. I don't want that to happen again.

Suggestion:

- Don't panic. Everybody forgets something sometimes. When you pause because your mind has gone blank, look at your audience and say something like, "Let me see if I've forgotten anything," or "Let me see what I can add to that," and then walk back to the lectern to check your notes. *The audience will only think it's a problem if you do.* If you accept the silence, and say something like "Oh yes, here it is," you can continue your speech and no one will hold it against you.

3. I don't know what I'll do with my hands.

Suggestions:

- It's time to start thinking about just what you *do* with you're hands when they're empty. When we stand, usually our hands fall to our sides with our fingers loose and slightly bent. *That's fine*, believe it or not. You'll also be punctuating your words with natural hand gestures.
- It's okay to occasionally fold your hands behind your back or in front of you, but for less than a minute, please. You need your hands for "talking," too.

4. I won't know where to stand.

Suggestions:

- Keep your knees loose, or one knee slightly bent. Don't "lock" them.
- Don't slouch.

- Don't stand at attention.
- Don't pace back and forth. *Too much* movement or repetition of a particular movement will disturb an audience.

5. I might trip.

Suggestions:

- Know your territory before you speak there. Scan the front of the room and aisles for that extra step down, a wire, or a worn carpet corner.
- The likelihood of your tripping is more a product of your own fears about the entire experience. Replace negative thoughts with positive ones, like "This is a pleasant room, and the people coming in look like they want to hear what I'm going to say."

6. Everybody will be staring at me.

Suggestions:

- They will be *watching* you, not staring, and they'll be waiting for your next words.
- Be comfortable with what you're wearing, while at the same time creating a physical image with your appearance. Your clothes should reflect your good taste, and a sense of authority and organization. For men, that often means a *jacket and tie.* For women, a blazer or a dress with classic lines and a modest hemline. No one *need* wear grey because it's considered the number one neutral, conservative color. It is true that muted, neutral colors—like navy blue, olive, camel, etc.—are best, though. Men can wear a tie that's brighter, as long as it's not too crazy. Women can add personality with a colorful scarf or chunky necklace (no noisy bracelets, though).

Have you ever taken an academic course that was on videotape? Many of us have. We have listened to professors who did excellent research in their field and who offered substantial material. But it was all on videotape, so I squirmed in my seat the whole time once

I got there. The *intended message* those professors gave me was important and well-planned, just as yours should be at all times. But the physical impact of an active, breathing human being—the *actual message*—was missing from the tape. The speaker didn't really know I was there.

Hints to Remember

- Achieving good physical delivery really means that you know your audience is there, waiting for contact from another human being.

- Movement away from the lectern is the key to achieving that contact.

CHAPTER 15

"Stuff"

Visual Aids

One way of making your speech easy to follow is to emphasize important ideas. A visual aid can help emphasize (as well as simplify and explain) important ideas. In this chapter, we will be discussing principles to follow when designing and using your visual aids.

Principles in Design of Visual Aids

Whether your visual aid is an object or a representation of an item, incident, or idea (such as a drawing, graph, photograph . . .) , *it should embody four qualities: it should be simple, colorful, large enough to see easily, and it should deal directly with the "heart" of your talk (**your main idea**).*

By creating an uncomplicated, *simple* visual aid, you allow your audience to concentrate on what you are saying—which is certainly more important than the object itself. Your visual aid is just that—an aid, an assistant, *a helper.* Spend your time (and our time) on your ideas. If we must take a long time (even ninety seconds can be a long time) to understand your visual aid, we have lost your talk's 'train of thought.' *Your visual aid's station in life is to quickly illustrate a key idea.*

Color adds not only interest to your visual aid; it also helps us to easily understand its different parts. A diagram explaining a company's power structure could color-code the different levels in the chain of command so that the viewer can quickly distinguish the separate sections.By the way, many schools' computer centers have software which allows you to create your own charts and graphs. Once printed, these items can be enlarged and/or made into overhead transparencies and then colored.

When creating your "assistant," be sure that it and its parts are *large* enough to be seen by all members of your audience. If, for example, you have included labels on a diagram, *write those labels large enough so that they are easily read by someone in the back of the room*—otherwise your assistant is an irritating block to communication.

The fourth principle in the design of a visual aid is that the object *relate directly to the heart of your speech.* Perhaps you are explaining the principle behind job-search networking. Your main idea is that networking improves your chances of finding out about unadvertised job openings by putting you in contact with people who travel in different "circles," different groups of people, than you do. Your visual aid might be a drawing of a few airplanes over different parts of the horizon, with one individual (the job-seeker) on the ground, in communication with the various pilots. In this case, your visual aid is a visual metaphor which helps us understand and remember your central idea.

Principles in the Use of Visual Aids

A well-designed "visual" deserves to be properly presented (a poorly-designed visual deserves to be left outside the room). Some guidelines in the use of visual aids include:

- Use a "moderate" number of visuals.

- Avoid blocking our view of the object.

- While you are showing us the visual, you should make sure that we are looking at that object. How? Easy: *you should be looking at (and talking to) us.*

- As simple as your visual may be, take a moment to *explain it to us,* so that you are sure that we understand it.

- Do not hand out your visual aid until your speech is finished (that is, unless you are trying to sabotage your talk with some clever interference . . .)

- If need be, and if permissible and possible, arrange the seating before the speech so as to facilitate your audience's view of your visual(s).

- *Practice* with your visual aids, preferably in the location and at the time of your speech. (Assume, for example, that you plan to show a few slides (transparencies) during a 2 PM speech. What would you do if during the delivery of the talk you discovered that super-nova mid-afternoon sunlight obliterates your projection through a window without shades?)

- Plan for emergencies (have, for instance, a spare projector bulb, just in case.)

- Show us the visual aid *only for the time you are referring to it; once you are finished using it, put it away* ("out of sight, out of mind").

What benefits do you garner when you have effectively used a well-designed visual aid? You and your audience reach an improved understanding of, memory of, and belief in your ideas.

Hints to Remember

- Be sure that your visual aids are simple, large, and colorful.

- Design your visual aid so that it reinforces your central idea.

- Practice using your visual aids in the same conditions in which you will be delivering your speech.

CHAPTER 16

Student Teacher

The Informative Talk

In an informative talk, your goal as speaker is to **teach**; *to report/explain/describe information which is* **new** *for your particular audience.*

Focus on your audience throughout the development of your teaching speech; *help that audience understand and remember your information by making your speech interesting, valuable, and easy to follow.*

Interesting Information

Begin preparing your talk by analyzing the interests and knowledge of that audience (see Chapter Three). *Present information which is unknown,* which is *new* to us. "New" can refer to an unusual topic or to a unique combination of previously unrelated ideas: ways in which space-age materials can be used to create new fashion designs. . . ingenious applications for computer-generated animation in a court case . . .

Novel ideas can be discovered as you investigate details. In other words, *Be specific.* By analyzing one feature of one element of one part of a single subtopic, you have a better chance of being more informative, more believable, and more interesting. Instead of explaining e-v-e-r-y-t-h-i-n-g about, let's say, day care centers, use your verbal microscope to explain the importance not of day care centers, not of those centers in a small business, not of the room sizes in those centers in a small business, but of the type of lighting used during the winter in large-room day care centers in small businesses. If a speaker tells her or his audience something that the audience already knows, then the speaker is not informing the audience; he or she is only boring them.

A part of analyzing what the audience knows about your topic involves discovering what *topic-related concepts and vocabulary they are familiar with*. For example, if you are going to discuss the stock market with a group of fresh-out-of-high-school college students, you may want to design your speech around an explanation—in everyday English—of basically how the stock market works, or what "stock" is.

Sure, some *jargon* may be "obviously" difficult, such as "stock," "industrial average," or "jargon" (oh, okay, "jargon" = "technical language"). However, other unknown terminology may not be so apparent. Many words which we use almost daily may have vague meanings. When considering foods, for instance, what does the word "lite" mean? In business, what is an "American" car? What constitutes "sexual harassment"?

Clearly and concisely define key words in "everyday English" (which means that you may have to translate the "formal" definition into good ol' American English). This way, you help avoid a situation in which language interferes with communication. For example, if you were to use the term "surrogate," you might consider giving your audience a dictionary definition: "a device used in lieu of the originally-intended unit." That, however, is more confusing than the term itself. Translated into everyday English, your definition might be: "a substitute."

Valuable Information

The interest shown by your listeners is also dependent on how important those listeners consider your information to be. Here, we begin considering the *value* of a talk.

Make sure that your ideas pass the *"So What?" test*, which we listeners tend to apply to talks (whether those are lectures or dinner table chats). Your listeners are asking "What's in it for me?" Tell us why your speech is important to us: what we will "get out of it?", *how we will benefit?*

Yet another part of your talk's value is linked to your sources; that support material which was discussed in Chapter Nine. Use information which comes from sources that we consider to be knowledgeable, unbiased, and *recent*. (Limit your use of books. Concentrate on current newspapers and magazines.) As you discuss information you have discovered, document those sources; mention and explain who those sources are and why they are believable.

By sharing your sources with us, you help to improve your own credibility in at least two ways: You are linking your credibility with that of authorities on the subject (this bolsters your competence and trustworthiness) and you are indicating to your listeners that you respect their intelligence.

Easy-to-Follow Information

Your credibility can be further enhanced by making your speech easy to follow. Use these five principles to help ensure that your speech will be easy to follow:

- **Know what you want to say.** See Chapter Seven.

- **Organize and outline your information.** See Chapter Eight(!)

- **Research your information.** See Chapter Nine.

- **Practice two principles of learning** (you are, after all, a teacher!). They are:

a. Emphasize important ideas. You can do this through the use of *repetition*. In addition to providing internal summaries, you can confidently use repetition by *previewing* your main points in your introduction, restating them in your talk's body, and then reviewing them in the conclusions.

b. Linking known information with unknown (new) information. In describing the way in which a microwave oven works, for example, a speaker might compare the quick rubbing together of hands for warmth with the much quicker rubbing together in the microwave of food molecules for much greater warmth.

An interesting, valuable, and easy-to-follow informative speech can be understandable and memorable for each listener—and for you, the teacher.

Hints to Remember

- Be Specific.
- Be able to say, in one sentence, why your information is *important to your particular audience.*
- Simple is beautiful: design your speech so that it is easy to follow.

CHAPTER 17

Why Should I?

The Persuasive Talk

A vacant lot came under city ownership, and Sally, a housewife and mother, had a great idea: why not build a playground on the site? She went to the next town meeting and proposed the idea. "The children need a place to go instead of hanging around the street," she said, and "I'm sure other families will feel the same way." Yet the City Council voted against it! What happened? One councilman wanted to know how much this playground would cost. The head of the PTA asked if it would be supervised, or if the children would just be hanging out there causing trouble. The proposal finally died, though, when the President of the Chamber of Commerce pointed out that downtown businesses would profit by building a new parking lot to encourage downtown shopping.

Sally stood up and told people her opinion. That takes courage. But when you speak to persuade, your opinion may be just one among many. As Sally learned the hard way at the City Council meeting, *merely stating your opinion isn't enough.*

So what about Sally's dream of building a new playground? She could try to get a group of parents together to petition and start to fight the opposition—*or she could take a look at her opponents' ideas.* Aren't they the people she's trying to persuade? Exactly! Before she attends the next City Council meeting, *she should try to find ways to satisfy her critics.*

Sally's first attempt failed because *she had no credibility* (see Chapter Two). The other parents believed in her plan, but her audience was the City Council and interested citizens, not just parents. If she had addressed their concerns *on their terms* and solved *their* problems, she might have been more successful. That is the bottom line with persuasion—*your arguments must sway not the speaker, but the audience.*

The Logical Argument

If you're speaking to persuade your classmates to always wear
their seat belts, you could find some stories about people whose lives
were saved by seatbelts. Have you made your case? Not yet, because
someone could relate a story where an accident victim was thrown
clear to safety because they *weren't* wearing a seatbelt! Now what?
It's your story against their story! To make a logical case, you will
need to research statistics and expert testimony to demonstrate that
while there may be an occasional exception, most people will benefit
from seatbelt use, and in fact may save their lives (review Chapter
Nine on Support Material).

Be sure you *stick to the facts*, avoid simply sharing your opinion, and use proof that will be accepted by your audience. For
example, if you cite as proof your interpretation of the Bible, that is
only valid to an audience that shares your particular religious
views—and they probably already agree with you, so they don't need
to be persuaded!

Here are some common mistakes in logic, known as *"fallacies."*

- **Generalization:** "Joe, Sue and Niki cut classes a lot, therefore all students want to do is goof off." While it may be
  true that Joe, Sue and Niki cut often, it doesn't follow that
  all students are goofing off, since Joe, Sue and Niki are just
  three students out of thousands.

- **Attacks on Character (real or invented):** "Senator
  Johnson's proposal for a new homeless shelter should not
  be adopted, since we all know he's getting treatment for
  alcoholism." While the Senator may have some personal
  problems, they are not sufficient grounds for ignoring his
  views on helping the homeless. *Labeling people* is related
  to this fallacy.

- **Insufficient Evidence/Choices:** "I ate a garlic pizza, and
  the next morning my cold was gone! Garlic must be the
  cure for the common cold!" There are many factors that
  could have contributed to this cold being cured. Related to
  this fallacy is *limiting choices*. "Either we stop immigra-
  tion completely or our entire society will be destroyed!"
  There are, of course, many other possibilities.

- **Dubious Premise:** If your initial assumptions are false, then any conclusions drawn from those assumptions will also be false. "San Francisco is about 100 miles from Houston, so we can drive there in a few hours." Yes, if the original premise were true, but Houston is much further than 100 miles from San Francisco.

- **Overstating the Case:** Another name for this error is lying! Speakers sometimes feel that they are justified in exaggerating their case a bit so that their speech will really make an impact. This is a grave error; your critics will attack your excesses—and they'll be right! Your whole speech may be discredited. *Stick to the actual facts.*

Writing the Persuasive Talk

With all the things you need to address in delivering a successful persuasion speech, how do you coordinate it? There are some common sense ways, such as outlining the problem and presenting your solution, or comparing the advantages of various actions, or simply stating your reasons. But perhaps the best way was developed by Alan Monroe of Purdue University: the Motivated Sequence. The beauty of this method of organization is that it follows the natural thought processes of an audience. You've probably heard speeches that started with a bang, and then dragged on and on until the speaker finally delivered the conclusion. This system keeps the audience involved from start to finish.

- **Attention.** As in any speech, grab the audience's attention at the beginning of your introduction. Get them interested in hearing what you have to say.

- **Need.** What's the problem? Let them see the current situation that needs correcting. Be sure to examine this from the perspective of the audience. This is the reason you're speaking on this topic!

- **Satisfaction.** Just when your audience wants to cry, "Isn't there anything we can do?!" you present your resolution and explain how it will solve the problem. Many speakers will stop here, but effective speakers will continue to the next step.

- **Visualization.** They're listening; hook 'em! Show your audience what will happen if they adopt your proposal. What's in it for them? This is your chance to put things on a positive note.

- **Action.** Perhaps you've delivered an eloquent speech, and perhaps your audience recognizes this and appreciates it, but it won't be worth anything unless you convince them to take action. Tell them specifically what action you want them to take, or nothing can change. Be prepared to give specific instructions and make it as easy as possible for your audience to take action. Prepare a petition, distribute a pamphlet, let them know where to go for more information, whatever, just be sure that they take action.

Hints to Remember

- Address the problems and concerns of your audience.

- Examine your logic to be sure you've made your case.

- Get your listeners to take action!

CHAPTER 18

The Skill of a Lifetime

Impromptu Speaking

Picture yourself sitting placidly in a classroom or business meeting. You are half listening, half drifting, as the speaker continues. Suddenly, you are uncomfortably aware that all eyes are on you. The speaker asks you again, "What are your thoughts on this?"

Whether you realize it or not, you have just been caught unprepared to give an impromptu speech.

"Wait a minute," you protest. "Maybe I wasn't paying attention—but, no one can prepare to give an impromptu speech. After all," you point out smugly, "an impromptu speech, by definition, is one given with little or no time to prepare."

Yes . . . and no.

This chapter will help you learn to prepare to speak impromptu. While it is true that you may not know with certainty the exact topic on which you may be asked to speak, you *can* prepare in several ways to be ready to speak on whatever is asked of you. You will learn to combine the skills you have learned from a lifetime of impromptu speaking with the public speaking skills you have more recently acquired to become comfortable in impromptu speaking situations.

You give a brief impromptu speech every time you answer a question or offer a comment in class. Most of what you say in any interview situation is impromptu speaking. So, although you may have had no formal training in impromptu speaking, you have had lots of practice. That's a good start. But, how can we make it better?

Preparation

Strong impromptu speaking begins with strong preparation. Here's how to prepare:

- **Know Your Stuff.** Face it. Most often, you are called on to give an impromptu speech by a teacher or by a boss because they believe that you have something valuable to contribute on the topic. So, by 'knowing your stuff,' you are beginning your preparation. For example, if a teacher assigns a chapter to be read for class, by having read the chapter, you are in a much stronger position if called on to comment. If your employer has asked you to 'look into' a subject, by doing the necessary research, you are ready to respond, if asked.

- **Anticipate.** As much as you'd like not to think about it, there are usually indicators that you might be called upon to speak. If a professor is in the habit of calling on students in class to comment on assigned material, then the assignment that reads, "Read Chapter 10 for discussion on Monday" is a big clue that you may be called on for comments. Likewise, if you are involved in an ongoing departmental project at work and you are attending a departmental meeting, you can anticipate that you are likely to be asked for a progress report. Further, if an agenda is sent to you for an upcoming meeting, use that list of topics to be covered to study and prepare.

- **Organize.** Having anticipated the likelihood of being called on and having prepared by 'knowing your stuff', you are now in a position to organize your material. Again, you are probably wondering how you can organize when you don't know what the exact question or topic will be. But, again, this is something you've been doing all of your academic career. Think back to your last exam. You knew the general subject matter that would be the focus of the test, but you didn't know exactly what questions would be asked. So you outlined your material, reviewed your notes, focused especially diligently on the areas you anticipated were most likely to be covered. (You *did* do all of this, didn't you?!) You organize your material in a similar manner for impromptu speaking. You anticipate that you will be called on and you anticipate *what* you are most likely to be asked about. Then, you ask yourself, "What do I most want my audience to know about this topic?" In other words, you *formulate a main idea*. Because an impromptu speech should be brief (more on this later), you might also want to consider only one or two main points that support your main idea.

- **Make Notes.** Here we are not suggesting that you write a speech. But just as you outline your text material or class notes for a final exam, you would also jot down the ideas formulated above. If you are in a meeting at work, you should take notes as you listen to presenters, not only to enhance your listening skills (remember the opening situation in this chapter!), but also because you can refer to those notes when called upon to speak. (again, we will discuss that further ahead in this chapter.)

- **Use a Standard Format.** Find an outline system that works for you and stick with it. Good written and spoken materials follow a pattern. In the broadest terms, material will have an introduction, a body, and a conclusion. As you make notes on text material or listening material, try to be aware of the format and take your notes accordingly. You will use this same broad format when organizing your thoughts for your impromptu speaking. Likewise, your introduction to an impromptu speech will ideally include attention-getting material and orienting material. The body of the speech will include one or two main points with support (if at all possible). The conclusion will briefly summarize your main points and reinforce your central idea.

Pitfalls of Impromptu Speaking

Ironically, as much as some dread impromptu speaking, *the biggest problem is getting the impromptu speaker to stop talking.* Afraid to miss a vital point and caught off guard, some impromptu speakers will babble on indefinitely. Cardinal Rule Number One is: *Be brief!*

Another major pitfall is *repetition.* If you have listened carefully to the other speakers, you will be able to avoid making points that have already been made. However, it is sometimes an appropriate technique to acknowledge what another or others have said previously, either to agree with or to take exception to their points. For example, you might say, "Ann previously made the point that our sales figures are a good indicator of the success of our marketing strategy. I agree in part with that, however, I would like to add two other factors."

If you have mentally organized the points you wish to make, you will avoid repeating yourself.

Yet another important rule is to *stay on topic*. Some speakers get so carried away with being the center of attention or are so disorganized that they talk about everything but what they have been asked to speak on. Keep your comments directly related to the point you wish to make and save the interesting stories for the social hour.

Advantages and Disadvantages of Impromptu Speaking

You may see absolutely no advantages to speaking impromptu, but, believe it or not, there are a few. Consider the fact that, because everyone knows you've been asked to speak 'off the cuff', *your audience does not expect a long nor highly polished speech*. Therefore, when you end up giving a concise, well-structured presentation with no apparent preparation, *your audience will be dazzled*. A decided advantage to learning how to become comfortable with impromptu speaking is that you will be a much better position to make your opinions heard in professional and other situations. And, the more practice you have in organizing your thoughts quickly, the better your become in all areas of public speaking.

The major disadvantage of impromptu speaking is that *you simply cannot give the speech topic the research and attention to detail that the topic may deserve*. Another common disadvantage is that there is a risk of *leaving out key information* when you are asked to give an impromptu speech. Also, you do run the risk of not being prepared for the actual topic on which you are asked to speak, although this is not as likely to happen if you 'do your homework'.

"Well," you say, "what if I prepare diligently and I'm still asked to speak on a topic that I don't know anything about?" Here's what Mark Twain said about that situation in his *Life on the Mississippi*: "I was gratified to be able to answer promptly, and I did. I said I didn't know."

Hints to Remember

- Impromptu speaking requires you to prepare, to listen, to organize quickly, and to use all of the oral and physical delivery skills required in any public speaking situation.

- Your impromptu speech should be brief and to the point.

- Gain confidence from the fact that you have had years of practice in impromptu speaking, just from asking and answering questions.

CHAPTER 19

A Conclusion (sorta . . .)

This is really not a conclusion, but the proverbial continuation. Perhaps you have already begun practicing various speaking and listening skills. You now consider your listeners more frequently and more in depth. Vocal variety intensifies your discussions in subtle, yet appreciated ways. Your daily conversations organize themselves more effectively. You can more insightfully analyze the messages and intents of others.

Constant improvement in these skills develops by focusing on one specific skill for awhile and honing it, then choosing another skill and polishing that one, and so on. The beauty of learning this group of skills is that improvement is not only unlimited, but it is free. You need no special equipment, just the basic concepts and the individual inclination to practice and experiment.

Effective speaking contains a paradox: one of the principles of this field is that effective speakers are audience-centered. And yet, by studying your listeners and by practicing the many ways in which they are receptive to your ideas, you begin developing a different way of seeing yourself. You realize that you can accomplish many feats—and you learn to believe in yourself.

CHAPTER 20

A List of Our Most Valuable Hints

After reading all of this, we hope that you've gotten to know us a bit. We like to think of ourselves as practical, rather than theoretical teachers of speech. As such, we often find ourselves giving students *hints*, rather than lectures, on how to improve their speaking skills.

We thought we might end on the same note, and give you the hint that we each feel is the most important hint for succeeding in a formal talk. We may have mentioned these hints elsewhere in the text, but since repetition is a teacher's stock in trade . . .

Hint #1

Plan ahead of time. Preparing for a speech is a step-by-step process that takes time and organization.

Prof Margot Papworth

Hint #2

Preparation is absolutely essential for consistently good public speaking.

Prof. Maryrose Eannace

Hint #3

Don't panic.

Dr. Kathy Barbour

Hint #4

Tailor your speech to the needs and concerns of your audience.

Prof. Tim Emerson

Hint #5

Don't treat the audience like a group of faceless objects; look at them, and have a conversation with them.

Prof. Carol Radin

Hint #6

In all instances—topic choice, preparation, writing, and delivery—**be sincere**. The biggest danger to any speaker is the fact that while audiences will let a nervous speaker get away with mistakes, they will not **tolerate** a phony.

Dr. John Robert Greene

Hint #7

In order to continually improve your communication skills, dedicate yourself to being a professional student: inquisitively practice your skills by observing others, learning from what they do well and learning from new ideas; apply supposedly unrelated ideas together.

Prof. John Suarez

Hint #8

Practice, Practice, Practice. And when you think you've got it right, practice *again*.

Prof. Paul MacArthur

Index

Reader Evaluation Form

As we noted in the beginning, we wrote this book for students like yourself. We are *very* interested in your comments, and we hope that you will take the time to write us with your thoughts. We guarantee that your ideas will be included as we update our work for future editions.

Please send this form to:

> *"The Speech*: An Evaluation"
> Cazenovia College
> Box F
> Cazenovia, NY 13035

Thank You!

_____Freshman _____Sophomore _____Junior _____Senior ___Grad

_____Faculty _____Staff/Administrator _____Personnel Professional

_____Other (Please Elaborate Below)

Class in Which *The Speech* Was Used:

School/College/University:

- General "Gut Response" to the Value of the Text:

- The Chapter that helped you the MOST, and WHY:

- The Chapter that helped you the LEAST, and WHY:

- A Topic that is MISSING, and Needs to be ADDED:

- Where You Think We Should EDIT (Too much written on an unimportant point):

- Other Messages or Thoughts to the Authors:

Optional:

Name _____

Address _____

Address _____